Belinda Blinked; Life Tips.
How to Buy the Best Property for You.

Authors;
Rocky Flintstone;
Belinda Blumenthal;
Bella Ridley;

Belinda Blumenthal, Bella Ridley and Rocky Flintstone sit down together and discuss how to purchase the best property available. This is one of their Life Tips series. It's really a concise guide to help you buy a home making sure it suits your way of living. Rocky gives you brief, detailed information to help you make the right choices. Bella asks the questions that need to be asked whilst Belinda comments on all the stuff we really need to know... or something like that...

Contents;

Foreword by Belinda Blumenthal;

Let's start our book by saying you should live where you want to but in doing so try to choose an area that will improve and will give you what you'll need in the near future. For example, if you want a decadent lifestyle such as Bella and myself, then choose wine bars and restaurants. If like Rocky and Wilma and you want to start a family, then choose an area with good schools.

Rocky makes the point that you could potentially make a lot of your money each time you buy a home… but only if you buy right every time.

Try to think outside the box… would an apartment be better than a fixer up house or vice versa? Bella and I love apartments or as our parents would call them… "flats!"

'Belinda… why do you think I would prefer a flat to a fixer upper house?'

'Because Bella my friend, you do not have a steady partner to help with the fixing up!'

'Belinda… what if I buy a fixer up flat… would you and Chiara help out with the fixin?'

'By the Norse Gods Bella… you do ask some awkward questions… but yes… so long as you provide the Chardonnay!!'

Look at all the possibilities within your budget provided they are in your chosen location. One of Rocky's early houses was originally in 2 flats.
'Belinda… I always knew Rocky was a bit stupid.'
Another one was an ex-dentist's premises.
'Belinda… that surely proves it…'
Another was very run down… Rocky learnt how to build!
'Pity he didn't learn to write at the same time…'
'Bella… stop it, Rocky doesn't need your criticism… just look at all those one star reviews of his books!'

What I'm trying to get across is that these are examples of unusual opportunities that can help you buy cheaply, make money and in time by moving upwards have a fine home.
A property needing a new roof and or major renovations are also areas to look at, but you will need to acquire new skills, time and or contacts.
'I would also advise being careful of taking on more than you can chew… it can easily end in disaster. I've had friends who've split up because of the stress and strain. Look at Des Martin… well perhaps not a friend… just a past acquaintance.'
'Don't you speak ill of my boss Belinda… I won't have it!'
'Sorry Bella… it's just an example of how things can turn out if you can't deal with fixing up your home.'

Be prepared to tackle jobs other people will not do as they are perceived as hard work. If you have the

cash like myself and Bella, then hire the professionals. If you don't have the dosh just like Rocky and Wilma... do it yourself!
'Belinda... surely Rocky's loaded... I mean he's one of the top UK based authors... right?'
'Mmmm... perhaps, but not when he was starting out.' Belinda replied.

Most people think stripping wallpaper is hard work... ('It is.' screams Wilma!!) so they will not contemplate doing really heavy work. Bella and I are in this category and we would hire a professional at a good price...
'Belinda... we could do a deal like that one you did with your camper van. You know, get a quote and negotiate with our assets until we've got a deal?'
'And Bella... what a deal that was...'
Bella laughed, 'Ha ha ha... and that's not even considering the rubbish collection man!'
'Yes Bella... fixing up properties always involves generating a lot of rubbish.'

When purchasing a property, you must be able to see beneath the existing exterior and onto the possibilities and opportunity that lies beyond it. It's like promoting or recruiting staff... do you see Bella's potential or is all just a smokescreen?
'Belinda... I never smoked... and never will... if I remember rightly when the Duchess first took you to Zacharia's...'
'Bella, shut up, that was in the past... OK!'

Some houses or apartments cannot be improved, but most can... so don't purchase the Bella's!
'Belinda... I do not appreciate being associated with something that cannot be improved.'
'Bella, it's just for the book... of course you can be improved... just ask Natasha Biles... our Welsh training guru and her lovely Porsche car.'
Bella grunted and shut up.

Do not buy unless you have a plan...
'I Belinda Blumenthal, always have a plan and so should you.'
'Belinda... what do you mean always have a plan?
'Bella, if you are going to buy a property which is highly likely to be the most expensive thing you'll ever buy, you need to have a plan on how to do it. How to get your deposit, find the property, get a loan or mortgage and then moving in with any repairs needed and so on... you need to plan for all this!'

After you have secured your loan or mortgage make sure you have easy access to the cash needed for any renovations you may want to make. Myself and Bella have good jobs and as such good access to ready cash in our monthly pay checks. If you're not so fortunate just as Rocky and Wilma had to, you will need to save in advance. By having a plan, you will succeed in buying the best property for you.

Introduction by Rocky Flintstone;

Should you buy or not?
With all the usual problems in the property market in most of the developed world this is a good question. However, as government becomes more rapacious through increasing property taxes, is it better to rent? Unfortunately, the answer is no, as these increasing taxes are rapidly passed on by landlords to their clients… you. Unless you are "moving on through" an area, then buying is for the best.
Most of us aspire to owning our own home as did Wilma and I; a place to have roots. Belinda will get to this stage of her life soon as she now has many responsibilities as the head of the Herstellung. Bella may never, but when she does settle down things will change for her too.

There are also issues concerning the lack of long term security if you are renting. This is less relevant today as various governments are attempting to improve the renter's rights. But there always remains that little bit of uncertainty. Belinda has also considered many times the quite huge cost of what can be seen as 'wasted money' going out on rent. So, remember although there are times when renting is best, this book is for those people who wish to buy their own home.
I with Belinda and Bella have designed this book to help you buy the best home, in the best place for your needs whatever they are. Let us help you

identify your needs first and your ideal property second.

Firstly, there are two things to bear in mind;
Most people have heard of Location, location, location.
We will add;
Research, research, research.
This is essential in order to get the best deal but it does take time and continual effort.
It used to be much harder when you had to physically visit the sales agent to see what was for sale, but now the internet is your research friend.
The facts are all available to you.
You just need to analyse them.
This can be easier said than done and information overload is a downer especially if like Belinda and Bella you have a high powered job and not much free time!

So be ruthless and drill down immediately to where you want to buy (location/area) and what type of property you want.

Location/Area;
You need to look at your own needs as this determines what you buy. Belinda wants to be close to the "Latin Quarter" in other words, trendy, hip, restaurants and entertainment. Wilma and I wanted

good schools, quality housing, robust policing and easy access to local amenities.

Remember different people have different needs for any area so write down your needs.

Think and analyse what you want and revise it constantly.

Do not fall into the trap of buying in the wrong area because the prices are lower thinking you will only stay there for a couple of years... you may never be able to leave it.

Learn the areas in your chosen town/city and develop accurate mental maps.

By studying real maps you will know where the various locations are... learn them!

You must also physically visit the areas you are initially interested in. It doesn't matter if they turn out to be a waste of time, a particular one may not be, it could be the real place you want to live!

I advise you to take the time and walk around them as you will observe much more than by driving through them. This process is called "Ground Searching" and is extremely essential. Belinda was only able to do this on a Sunday morning because of her heavy workload, but it became something she really enjoyed and still does it as she plans for her next property purchase. It is also important to be aware of the market in your chosen areas and know your prices and property types. By doing this you will be able to spot a bargain immediately. This is called getting your eye in.

Property type;
The size of property and type of property are determined by what you want and can afford.
Think about your possible purchase and then think of five years ahead to avoid getting trapped in the medium term. Is a two bedroom flat big enough for your future needs, or would you be better purchasing a small two bedroomed house?
'Rocky,' said Bella… 'I don't understand… they are both two bedrooms?'
'Bella, its all about size, a small house will have a garden, kitchen and lounge whereas a studio apartment will not have these extra amenities.'

An important point to consider is whether your salary will go up as your job prospects improve like Belinda and Bella's. Or are you happy with your job where you are now and want to purchase a property for your present needs which are unlikely to change much.
'So, Bella, as you will undoubtably be earning more money in the future, you could maximise your borrowings and purchase a more expensive property knowing the repayments will not be so arduous in a year or two because you will be earning more money. Got it?'
'Yes Rocky, I have, thank you.'

This all boils down to what is essential for you?

What can you compromise on?
But the million dollar question is; Are you planning on having children in the foreseeable future? They change everything. Remember it is often easier to buy then sell so purchasing something which is appropriate for your needs for the next five years is a no brainer; If you buy a small flat in a place with poor schools and no green spaces you may rue the day if you have children. This is why you have to have your own individual plan and you need to be honest about what you want and can afford.

Compromise;
You will also need to have some areas of compromise. Do you need a garage or just a garden? Not being able to compromise may make life harder for you in achieving your dream home. This relates especially to the type of area and the type of property you wish to purchase; Work it all out before you purchase, you'll find the decisions much easier to make.

Chapter 1

Area;

Your aim is to buy the best possible house in the best possible area for you.

A different person will read this book and make different choices. Bella will choose differently to Belinda... well she did when buying her horse riding outfit. She earned less money and so had to economise, but at the end of the day, they both went riding.

Here's another example; A brother and sister.

The brother is married and planning for children like myself and Wilma.

The sister is single and a career person like Belinda and Bella.

It's important to understand whilst they both live in a city their choices will be very different.

You can always find undervalued areas; you just need to know where to look.

You will need to take a small risk on the area developing for the better in the future but we will keep that risk as small as possible by using various techniques.

Your objective is to be at the cutting edge not the bleeding edge.

Look initially at where you want to live in a perfect world.

Can you afford it?

If yes, it is a simple decision.

Usually however it is no. Wilma and I found ourselves in this situation many times. It means that you will now need to look at other locations.

Look at where your family and friends live.
Then look at your distance to work.
Now look at the facilities you need.
Shops, cinemas, restaurants, bars, delis, coffee shops etc...
Again, different people have different priorities.
Belinda would prefer upmarket restaurants whilst Bella would like a good wine bar.
Belinda does not want to have to drive to her favourite restaurants every weekend and not be able to drink when socialising so it makes sense for her to locate as close to them as possible.

The problem is that good facilities attract more good facilities and so they tend to cluster.
It can be tiresome driving a long way as well as expensive and there is no doubt that the expense of travelling will get greater in the future so choose your area carefully. Also make sure you can get to work easily.

Transport links and schools are two very important variables in the mix for generating a future profit through property purchase. Areas with good local schools will command a higher price for the surrounding property and as such house prices will increase. Remember you make the profit when you

buy so look carefully. If you spend far too much you may never get it back.
Once you have all this information on facilities transport etc. get a map and look at all the areas you would like to live in.

Visit them in person to get a feel for the areas, never rely on friend's words of wisdom. Remember we all want different things for our ideal home. As I have previously said and I make no apology for repeating myself, this is called "Ground Searching" and is absolutely vital.
OK, I agree it's time consuming but there is not really a substitute. It's the only real way for you get a feel for the area and the type of land use it generates.

'What do you mean by "land use?"' asks Bella.
'Really good question Bella,' replies Rocky?
'Land use is a term which means what was the original land used for, was it...
Residential housing as in housing estates.
Commercial as in shopping centres.
Light industrial as in small industrial estates.
Heavy industrial such as in gas towers, ship building.
Mixed which can be a mixture of all the above, or just even two of the above.
Remember national and local government can decide to develop run down areas which may be worth investigating.
Brownfield sites in cities are where a government decides to turn old redundant industrial areas into

new housing. They are basically turning old brown coloured, polluted land into green residential spaces. It's good for the environment and local people.'

If you can't afford the best areas, move to their fringes until you can move closer in to a better property. You might find that you don't need to move in five years time as the area you choose on the fringe of a good area has become part of it. A real money making result for you!
When choosing on the fringe, analyse it, what does it feel like? Could you live there?
Wilma and I once visited an area that looked a good fringe area on the internet, but it was so run down there was no way it was going to improve in the next 20 years.

Main roads are often dividing lines for good and fringe areas. Try sticking close to these main roads but on the wrong side for a better price.
Non-residential land use nearby is another way to get a bargain. If the property is next to a garage or small warehousing it will be cheaper and in time those facilities may get knocked down and turned into decent housing.

The same is true for houses on busy main roads. Busy roads are noisy, but safe to walk along at night and have good bus links.

Consider installing double glazing in your initial budgets to overcome the noise levels... or negotiate it off the price of the house.
Choose what disadvantages you can live with.
Remember most negatives also have a positive.

Living opposite builder's yards or car service garages can be noisy and dusty, but it means you're not being overlooked by other residents. By factoring in these type of commercial disadvantages, you can get a deal because other people have dismissed them without thought.
Remember for an area to develop well in the future it will be close to good areas, with good property stock such as older, well maintained, buildings. You cannot really go wrong if you can discover these locations. Generally speaking, they were built from the 1890's onwards.
Good transport links and schools may come later when the demand from people buying them has grown.

Try to avoid areas with a lot of cheaply built local government property as they are much more difficult to maintain as they tend to have been poorly built in the first place.

Always remember you can only learn so much without visiting the area in person. Gut reaction is important but make sure it is correct and not an over-reaction. Think your way through the pros and cons.

'Rocky... sorry to butt in but can you clarify a pro and a con...?'

'Yes Bella... it's like any business deal we come across... the pros are the good points about the deal and the cons are the bad points. It's the same with property, there will be pros and cons.'

Your first impressions are not always correct but are influential so it does no harm in revisiting a possible area lots of times in the day and the night. Also, if possible, during weekends and week days. Be aware of the problems larger residential buildings can have. If a building is very big it can be prone to become rented out in bedsits or small units. They invariably were very good areas in the past, so may become so again, but the number of people renting them will affect the quality of life in the area. This can make it harder (but not impossible) to develop for the better. As a rough rule of thumb houses more than 3 stories high and with more than 6 bedrooms are indicative of this type of property use.

Look at the local shops. If there are lots of funeral homes then it is highly likely it has an ageing population which will mean a turnover of property as the population dies. Old people generally maintain their property well but they will need updating. These can be the best houses as they can be brought up to modern standards without too great a cost.

Look at the ethnic activity. If you are from a certain ethnic group and want to live near places of worship etc. then this may be your place to live. Are there coffee shops/tapas bars/ trendy wine bars/pubs close by. If this is the case, then this area is on the up. This is the land with a good future.
If not, it could be... but might not be... so be careful as you are buying what is there at the moment.
The future might be postponed or never happen. Local infrastructure may be promised, but never happen due to many factors.

Refuse skips are a good sign as it shows there is renovation going on and owners are spending money on their properties.
Remember some good areas are not always more expensive as they can be unfashionable.
Unfashionable is a hard word to explain... it is a gut feeling.
'Belinda and Rocky.... I need it explaining... sorry, but I've been good for a few pages now, so come on...'
'Fair enough Bella... Rocky?'

'OK let me explain.
In the 1980's old houses were unfashionable as they were hard to heat.
This was not helped by the spike in energy costs from the energy crisis in the 70's.

You could get a deal in 1980 on a British Victorian gem built in the 1890's worth 10 times less than now.
Even in bad property times this can still happen to your advantage.
1970's houses can be a good deal as they tend to be large but often ugly and thus unfashionable.'
'Thank you Rocky.' said Belinda.

When visiting your targeted areas look at the school uniforms as you can see whether the local kids are cared for or not.
What is their behaviour like?
Look at the traffic especially type and age of cars.
Look at the housing stock… is it well painted and maintained.
Are there modern shutters on the windows?
Off street parking?
Basement conversions?
Child buggies?
Attic conversions?
These are all signs of an improving housing stock. Or you can buy in the poorer areas and wait for them to improve.
If you get it right you can do very well indeed.

Once affluent areas fallen on harder times can be good options. Factories may have closed leaving the homeowners less affluent. The risk is they may not develop until new businesses are developed.
Can you take it as it is?

What about if you had kids?
How will you save yourself if it goes wrong?

Do not be only optimistic, be pessimistic as well.
PLANNING and ORGANISATION are the keys to
success.
Important variables are:-
1) Transport links;
2) School provision;
3) Politics through local and national government
input;
4) Population movements;

Transport;
If you get in well before any new link is developed
you will get a deal.
North London is generally more expensive because
of good transport links.
In the future fuel costs will rise more so make sure
you are not isolated or have a long commute.
Hefty toll road increases in the past cost some
residents 50 euros a day to go to work in Portugal.

Schools;
This is important because most people have kids and
private schools are expensive.
Good schools are what to look for. Try to find out
how various local schools compare to schools in
other parts of the city or indeed the country.
You want a good quality life with your kids look for
parks, activities etc.

If your kids can walk to school or nursery then you will have cheaper child care.

Politics;
Look at political issues like local government costs and taxes.
They all have different taxes and this can be important as they will impact on resale values.
In the USA consider property taxes.
Plans for the future can blight or make an area.
What do you know?
Find out by talking to local people and from local news publications.
Airports are important and very political.
You want to be near them, but not on the flight path.
Remember, in the future, we will need more airports and they will have to be built somewhere.

Population;
Population movements are vital.
Are people moving in or out?
You do not really want to be living in a declining area as house prices will deteriorate.
Live in an area which is on the up and property prices will tend to rise due to increased competition.
Do not end up in a dead area as you may never be able to sell no matter how cheap it is.
Old industrial areas fit this scenario.
Avoid 'rust belt' places such as Detroit in the USA and North East England.

Property values going down but taxes remaining high
are a lose-lose situation.
Also look at the competition, are there a lot of
houses/flats/apartments all the same size and price?
If so, they will make it harder to sell if you have
bought one of them in the past.

So, remember;
Do lots of research on the internet first.
Take photos and return at different times to ground
search.
Know your chosen area.

'So, Bella, once you've found the areas you're interested in, the next hurdle will be how can you afford the property you want?'
'I suppose I'll look for types of property that could be undervalued.'
'Good answer, I have to say you've been listening, well done! Yes, look at the market and know your prices and property types. Then you'll find the undervalued ones.'

There are many different ways to get a deal;
1.) Look at an ugly property and improve it.
2.) Go to the fringe of a good area.
3.) Look near non-residential land use.
4.) Look at a house that has been subdivided into flats.
5.) Look at commercial property that can be converted back to residential use.
6.) Look at total remodelling projects that need a lot of work.

At the end of the day your primary objective should be to be in the right area where you will have the facilities you can walk to with good transport links. Only you are in charge of making your property purchase work for you. Remember that it will be harder to sell in tough times but if you are moving on

to another property you will have the opportunity to negotiate a deal on that one.
'Please explain Rocky.'

OK Bella, if for example you are selling your apartment and the prospective purchaser only offers you 10% less than your asking price, you can go to the owners of the property you are purchasing and ask a similar percentage off their asking price. This is normal negotiation and all selling agents are used to it. The same is true if you are asked to reduce your properties sales price because a surveyor's survey has uncovered some problems. If your survey on the property you are purchasing uncovers a problem then you too can ask for a price reduction.
'Thank you Rocky... good thinking.'

It is important not take on more work than you can handle and do not pay too much for a property that needs a lot of work. Renovation is expensive and time consuming.

Have a list of property preferences or must haves and a written check list of these to which you can refer. You will certainly have to compromise on your property unless you have an awful lot of money. Your preferences should contain these general common points;

1. Off street parking; Is it essential? If you have children this becomes a lot more important

as you don't want to walk a long way with a crying baby and shopping.

2. Garden size; How much do you need?
3. Garage; Do you need this? Or want it?
4. Utility room; Again, is this a want or a need?
5. Extra bathroom; Could you add one if it is not already there?
6. Extra bedroom; Could you divide a large bedroom into two?

Decide what is essential for you and compromise on other things.

Buying a Fixer Upper Property;

To save money go for a dowdy property or one in poor condition. In the world of buying property this is known as having no "kerb appeal".

Don't let interior smells put you off as they will be coming from mostly carpets and soft furnishings which can be moved into a skip immediately you move in.

Take lots pictures for reference later.

Revisit the property at least once.

Plan ahead; What will you need to do to improve it?

Look at your pictures to confirm your thoughts.

Do not buy a small apartment if you are planning children soon because if you can't sell later on you might be stuck in unsuitable accommodation.

Do not borrow so much that the pips squeak... unless your income is going to increase in the near future.

Remember if you are renovating, you'll need cash for that.

The following are a list of advantages and disadvantages you need to have considered before you buy that particular type of property.

Buying Apartments and Flats;
There are many advantages to buying this type of property.
1. Easy to manage.
2. Cheap to run and heat.
3. In a community so safe.
4. No garden to organise.
5. They often have a balcony.
6. Cool and hip.

BUT
There are disadvantages also.
1. Small.
2. Cramped.
3. Less private.
4. Higher running costs with condo fees.
5. Little or no outside space.
6. Less good for children.

Buying older property;
Advantages;
1. Located in better areas.

2. Established transport links.
3. Schools nearby.
4. Wide range of facilities on hand.
5. Bigger rooms.
6. Bigger gardens.

Disadvantages;
1. Harder to heat.
2. Harder to maintain and you will have to pay for the work if you can't do it yourself.
3. Car parking can be a problem.
4. Money pit issues… they can eat up all your cash.
5. Can ruin your relationship unless you both agree on this course of action.

Buying new property;
Advantages;
1. Easy to run.
2. Cheap to run.
3. Well designed. Car parking.
4. Purpose built utility rooms.
5. Garage.

Disadvantages;
1. Located further out of town meaning, more travelling.
2. Similar houses all built together which can mean they are harder to sell.
3. Smaller gardens.

4. Not as attractive… lots of concrete and tarmac and not so much greenery.
5. Less good transport links which may take many years to be improved.
6. Less facilities.
7. Can be a long way from the established schools.

Locating in the City or Town;
Advantages;
1. Schools are better and there is a choice.
2. Less driving.
3. One car rather than two for a couple can be a big saving.
4. More independent kids…. they can walk to school.
5. Public transport links.
6. Leisure facilities.
7. Friends nearby.

Disadvantages;
1. Crowded.
2. Noisy.
3. Parking problems.
4. More expensive.

Locating to the countryside;
Advantages;
1. Quiet.

2. Peaceful.
3. Cheaper.
4. Bigger.
5. Pleasant lifestyle.

Disadvantages;
1. Poor transport links.
2. You will need 2 cars.
3. Expensive commutes.
4. You will have to drive everywhere.
5. You may never relax as someone has to drive
   for the kids.
6. Isolated.
7. Difficult in hard winters.
8. Few facilities.
9. Few choices.
10. Your social life might not be so exciting.
11. Few leisure facilities.

To sum up all the above you will need to decide the following...

1. What kind of property you want.
2. What type of condition are you happy with.
3. Choose between an apartment or a house.
4. What age of property.
5. What type of house.
6. What location... town, country or seaside.
7. Search for and find an undervalued house.

8. Consider locating near non-residential property.
9. Purchase on a busy road.
10. Buy an ugly with no kerb appeal property.
11. Buy a property which has been sub divided into flats/bedsits.
12. Purchase on the edge or fringe of the area.

These are jobs we can all do but be warned Belinda and Bella, it is hard work and sometimes it never seems to end. It can also be very messy, so wear your dungarees Belinda, not your riding gear Bella! For a time, you may have to live in terrible conditions... dust, cement, wallpaper peelings, soot to name but a few. The important thing is that you can do all this sort of basic work yourselves with only a bit of professional help. This will save money which can be used to buy other items.
Never do jobs you are not skilled for especially gas, electric or major building work such as removing walls. In these instances, you must get professional tradesmen in.

Improving the Garden.
This can add to the value and the enjoyment of any property. Plants and shrubs can make a big difference to any outside area no matter how small it is. Hard landscaping such as patios and outside dining areas will enable you to use these areas all year round. Consider having a BBQ area. It doesn't matter whether you prefer charcoal or gas, having somewhere set up ready to go will make you want to

cook outside. Fire pits are great for the cooler evenings and are very social. If you are hard paving a larger area, remember to account for the extra drainage of rainwater this will cause.

By completing these simple projects, you will add value to the property for just a bit of hard work and only a few materials.

Improving your Parking;

If the property does not have off street parking and you have the potential space, ask for planning permission to install it. Remember you will have to pay for the existing kerbs to be lowered as well as your own new driveway.

Adding a Conservatory;

This is the cheapest way to get an extra room but conservatories will require more heating in the winter months. On the other hand, they are wonderful in spring, summer and autumn. Placed in the correct place they can also extend the enjoyment of the garden into the home. Conservatories are also good for socialising or as a child's play room. Have a large box which can also be used as seating for overnight storage of the toys. This will retain your social space and not that of a playroom. If you are an advanced, do it yourself expert, there are many conservatory self-build kits in the market worth considering.

Improving the Kitchen;
You can replace the old jaded kitchen units and counters with new ones giving your kitchen a new lease of life. Remember you need a qualified tradesman to work on the electrics, gas and water. Using granite or a similar modern product for your work tops will give a wow factor and are pretty much indestructible. Whilst not the cheapest option they will last a long time and are very much worth the initial investment.
If money is tight, consider repainting the old units. Keep some of the paint as you will have to touch up due to the amount of use kitchen units experience. Good preparation and finishing is essential so use a specialised paint which will stand up to being wiped down a lot. Check it is also resistant to heat and steam from cooking. To help with this problem you could consider installing an extractor unit.

Install an ensuite bathroom;
This is always a big plus if you have the space in the biggest bedroom. Try not to make the ensuite too small as this will not add much value. Check out the local authority guidelines and permission if this is needed.

Improving an existing bathroom;

One good effective way is to tile it... both the floor and the walls. Seriously consider under-floor heating as it is not a great extra cost and makes walking on the tiles more comfortable in colder weather. A modern shower is very important but remember if you want to remain family orientated when selling you will need a bath. A bath is essential for young children but you can consider adding a shower to the bath if space is tight.

Install a downstairs toilet;
This is always a plus if there is room.... even consider under the stairs. If you use a macerating toilet be careful with its use as items such as string can foul the chopping blades and are difficult to fix, but not impossible. These units allow the installation of a toilet in an area with no external soil pipe. This is because the exit pipe it uses is much smaller, but it is easy to block so be careful with its use and always follow the manufacturer's instructions.

Replace the front and back doors;
Whilst this will be an additional expense it can add kerb appeal. Sometimes it can even make the house look a million dollars. The same is for new gates.

General exterior work;

Repainting the outside is another cheap fix. If you feel unsafe using ladders then get the experts in. Gentrify the outside using black and white Tudor beam effects if this is suitable for the house and area. Consider adding a porch to give interest to a bland looking house but check with the local authorities first. Replacing old and tired windows and installing new style interior shutters will improve the appearance of the property. These will look good, give extra security and can also hide an unappealing outside view.

Inside the property;
New, modern style down lighting can modernise a house instantly and cheaply (Wilma hates these) as can paint and redecorating. Choose classic shades and if it is an older property, heritage colours such as Farrow and Ball manufacture in the UK. Cream and off white does not date but can be boring so add brighter coloured accessories and choose classic furniture. Bland does not mean boring but do not try and have a hotel style look as it indicates that no one lives in the property. Avoid clutter and create storage to hide away essentials.

The following will save you money in the medium term but will entail an initial cash outlay.
Insulation;
A new boiler.

Installing a water meter.
So, Belinda and Bella are you game to get stuck into all these projects and save yourselves money? It really is your decision!
'Yes Rocky! shouts Belinda.
'Bring it on Rocky!' shouts Bella.

'Rocky, do you think Bella and I would be good at renovation?'
Belinda, that is a very good question, so let's go through what's entailed in a renovation project and we'll see what you both think once you've had all the pros and cons.

Renovation or remodelling is tough work so do not contemplate doing it unless you are well prepared. Before you finalise the purchase of a property which needs renovating, get a professional survey carried out on the condition of the property. This is quite expensive but with such properties extremely useful. The detailed survey will give you an idea of what you will need to work on and in which order. Replastering the wall of a room would not need to be completed immediately, but replacing old and broken drainage gutters would be a priority.

Often you will have to have work completed for the mortgage company such as rising damp and wall ties before they will advance all the loan monies. This is very normal for renovation projects. What usually happens is that they will withhold a portion of money until the requested work is completed and they have inspected it. In my experience the mortgage companies are very good at approving such works and getting your monies to you.

'Rocky, sorry to interrupt?'
Yes Belinda.
'You mentioned rising damp and wall ties... what are these?'
Good question Belinda. Rising damp is an area of the wall of the house where the old damp proof course has broken down and is no longer effective. Dampness is moving up the wall from the foundations and needs to be stopped. A qualified contractor will replace the old damp proof course or membrane with a new one. This will cure the rising damp problem. Wall ties are metal strips placed between the outer brick wall and the inner brick wall when they are being built giving it more strength. Unfortunately, over the years, these will rust and decay. A slight bulging of the wall may occur once they have lost their strength. These wall ties will need to be replaced and again a qualified contractor will need to carry out the work. You may need the invoices and guarantees for the mortgage or loan company, so keep them for future inspection.
'Thank you Rocky... very informative.'

When you purchase an older property there are some vital jobs which will need to be completed and the most important of which is replacing the electrical circuit breaker with a modern unit. This will protect your entire household from electrocution so again get a qualified electrician to do this work. As is the way with DIY, accidents do happen and a modern circuit breaker will save you a lot of bother from leaking electricity which is dangerous and can kill.

When you start your renovation work you will enter the initial phase which is basically the destruction of your new home. This will consist of hacking plaster off walls, sanding floor boards (try and leave this to the last as your newly sanded boards will suck in the dirt quicker than a sponge)
and stripping off old wallpaper. When you start this work, you will encounter further problems which will have to be fixed before you can make good again. Dry rot and wet rot and woodworm are pretty common and are very messy which can make you feel disheartened. If it's quite severe, it can cost a lot to fix, but the good news is they're not unbeatable. This is work a budding DIYer can do with modern day materials and chemicals designed for the job. Because of these potentially unknown problems it is always a good thing to only tackle a room at a time. You do not want the workload to overwhelm you. Remember everything is fixable but at a cost.

When you get the results of your property survey look for the following...
1. Roof problems;
2. Dry rot;
3. Subsidence;

4. Woodworm;

These are all potential major areas of cost, so get quotations for the work and negotiate to reduce the properties price.

Whilst you are living in a property being renovated it is worth considering the following.
1. Work on one room at a time thereby containing the mess.
2. Work on the hallways last as they will always get messed up with the other work being completed in the property.
3. Do not put down carpets until all the work has been completed.
4. Try to make your bedroom a haven. Complete the work here first so that you have somewhere pleasant to retreat to at any time of day.
5. Remember Rome was not built in a day and always keep going, you will get there!

Slavia Blumenthal awoke early. Her partner Tom had already left for work, again… sometimes Slavia thought he was more in love with his job than her. You see, he was a crane driver working in his father's business, but Tom didn't drive any old crane, his was high tech. The Goliath V69 recently imported from Texas was the first and biggest of its kind in the UK and Tom was its only fully trained operator.

Slavia turned over, her latest piece of work was fascinating her and she couldn't get the myriad of jigsaw pieces out of her mind. She was a criminal fraud specialist and two years ago she'd been headhunted by her current employer… a small group of virtually unknown accountants based in central London named Dribble, Drabble and Babbel. They specialized in forensic cyber fraud and her most recent case had resulted in their making her a junior partner. The first and, according to her boss Harry Babbel, the only.

You see Slavia had found the back door coding to a massive fraud committed on her cousin's company Steeles Pots and Pans. Belinda was the International Sales Director and had been distraught at the crime. She had divulged a lot of pertinent information to Slavia the last time they'd met up and her inside knowledge of the two perpetrators Sammy Quinn and D'Artangan Raspberry had sparked a train of thought which split open the case.

Everything except £200,000 pounds had been recovered, though all press releases stated everything had been accounted for, and the Head of MI6, the mysterious Duchess, was seemingly very impressed at the partners success. More work had flowed in from MI6 but the missing £200K still bothered Slavia and whilst the accountant, Sammy Quinn, was now dead, she knew that D'Artagan Raspberry the ex-Financial Director at Steeles, would again raise his head in the near future.

Slavia dressed in a thong and skimpy T-shirt, went downstairs to make a pot of tea and start another days work. Two hours later her front doorbell rang, it was the postman who handed her a registered parcel.
'Looks like a smallish book Miss,' he suggested, 'looking her closely up and down, just sign here please.' As he left, the postman decided he'd get put onto this round permanently.
Intrigued Slavia went into the kitchen and carefully opened the small parcel with a very sharp knife. Her boss Harry, hadn't told her to expect anything, so who was this from?

Slavia burst out laughing, she couldn't help it… the book was from Belinda with the title of, "How to buy

Slavia smiled.
Finally, after years of saving, she was going to get her
hands on a house…
She turned over in the under sexed king size bed and
adoringly stroked the naked back of Tom, her long
term lover, who was still asleep next to her. He had
proposed marriage to her last night… and she had
immediately said, "Yes…YES… and YES! again!"

Slavia salivated.

She and Tom celebrated their new earthly union
later that morning in another, more conventional,
way by browsing through houses for sale online.
Belinda's book had told them it would save them a
lot of shoe leather. They had finally decided it was
time to get their own place and leave behind the
uncertainties of renting. Besides, they had to put
Belinda's book to the test and who better to do it
than Slavia herself.
"Who would have thought that property could be so
sexually arousing when my cous writes the book?"
she wickedly thought.
Slavia mused, turning to Tom and continued now
somewhat sexually aroused,

"Come on, you girthy buyer, get that meaty chimney of yours out and light up my fire irons."

Tom and Slavia engaged in some deeply passionate penetration for the next six minutes, until Slavia had an idea. Tom's pulsating love newel post always gave her inspiration. She pulled back from his rapidly diminishing walnut wand and cried,
"Let's sort out our mortgage broker and ring one right now!"
"But we're both totally naked!" Tom winced.
"Who cares, Tom? It's not a video call or anything… possibly, let's do what Belinda would do and get a mortgage!"

Slavia had already researched the mortgage facilitator market, small as it was, in their neck of the woods and made Tom make the call.
"Bruce Clapworthy here. How may I assist you?"
The voice was trustworthy yet boring, and convinced Tom to press on with his and Slavia's fervent desire to purchase a property.
"Hi, Bruce. My fiancée and I would like a mortgage to buy our dream bungalow."
Tom grinned across at Slavia who was lazily pulling at her mahogany-coloured nipples, and they high-fived each other with their bare feet.

Tom quickly answered Mr. Clapworthy's questions about their salaries and employment situations: he operated large, powerful cranes, whilst Slavia

worked as a Cyber Detective, specialising in financial fraud.
As the broker's voice cracked just a little bit at Slavia's job he managed to drone on. Tom felt Slavia's hands slowly creeping over him and finally exploring his fleshy joist, gently massaging the sweating folds like a pizza chef preparing dough for cooking. Perhaps mortgages weren't so boring after all... if you were with the right person...

Bruce had just started to explain the intricacies of interest rates when Slavia's hands suddenly clenched down onto Tom's veiny drainpipe, like an over-eager claw machine at the penny arcade. Tom groaned.
"A fine piece of real estate you've got there, Thomas," Slavia grinned wickedly,
"Just the right size for a first-time buyer."
Her downstairs love furnace sparked furiously with anticipation as she continued to toy with him.

"I do hope the deposit you've been saving up is big enough to meet the requirements." continued Bruce in Tom's ear.
Tom nodded eagerly as he reached a hand towards Slavia's shapely calves. She swatted him away with a knowing smile before slowly opening her legs to reveal a glimpse of her glistening whirlpool of desire.
"I need to be sure that this buyer won't pull out and leave me disappointed..." whispered Slavia.

Tom groaned. If his lengthening todger had been a wolf, it would have been howling at the moon... never mind the door...

Suddenly Mr Clapworthy's voice took on a more excited tone.
"Now, here's the good news: I've done the math's and you pair qualify for a mortgage of £315,000, and the lender will be FLAPPS Investments PLC. In this instance their five-year fixed-rate mortgage gives you the best rate, and allows you to remortgage after the initial fixed period has ended. You should qualify for that without any problems, provided your financial documents are in order, blah blah blah..."

"God, I'm so wet." Slavia muttered. No one had ever mentioned that mortgages were so exciting... not even Belinda's book. Her mysterious juice soaked pleasure-bean vibrated with even more anticipation. Tom looked longingly over at Slavia, he could read her like a mortgage proposal, his hardwood substructure twitching as if waking from a confusing dream. He wanted to devour her like a late-night chicken burger meal deal without the interest rates. Seeing the hunger in his eyes, Slavia opened her legs even wider, waggling her now extended nipples at him alluringly before purring,
"You can climb my personal property ladder anytime you like sweetheart."

Broker Bruce's voice cut through the sexual tension like a cordless drill.

"And finally, I'll confirm your mortgage application will be started with FLAPPS by next week. They have an online portal for ease of use, so you can just upload anything to the hub as and when you have it. Will that be all for today?"

Slavia sighed, frustrated. All the promised sweaty action would have to wait. However, on the bright side, property buying was turning out to be much more fun than she had expected... even with Belinda's book at her side.

"Shall we get dressed and research the area for our dream bungalow?" Tom asked after the call had ended.

"As long as we get to try before we buy," Slavia quipped, winking extensively.

Tom grinned. With Slavia and her little book at his side, what could go wrong?

Slavia salivated;

Over the next few days Tom and Slavia ground searched the property market in search of their dream home. Try as they might, there was nothing in Girthington-on-Sea that fulfilled their sexual desires for their own bungalow.

"Everything we've found so far has reminded me of you after a few beers," said Slavia with a grin.

"Poorly maintained?" Tom replied.

"Disappointing and flaccid." laughed Slavia.

"And what about that one with the awful basement? It was almost as damp as you!" Tom added wickedly.

As they curled up in bed that night, Slavia exhaled in frustration. It was turning out to be much harder than she had expected, and not in a good way, even with the wise words of Belinda running around her head... "research, research, research; ground search, ground search, ground search."

Slavia continued the search during her lunch break the next day. She tirelessly scrolled through listing after listing until her jaw dropped. She'd found it: a three-bedroom bungalow with a ferociously large extension and private bushy gardens. At £350,000, even the price was right... if a bit tight.

She discarded her half-eaten meal deal and scooted back into her makeshift office as fast as she could. 'Tom has got to see this, pronto, she thought'. Sitting down in the cubicle, she dialed Tom's office.
"Slingshot Crane Hire. Our cranes, your erections," the elderly receptionist answered tiredly.
"Mavis, it's Slavia. Can you get Tom to pick up his mobile?"

Two minutes later Tom was on the line.
"Tom! Can you talk?" Slavia burbled breathlessly.
"Yep. Give me a second to get to the cab of my Luffing Jib 69, where I'll be reasonably private."
"I've found it! Our bungalow… I'm sending you the link now."
Tom's phone vibrated immediately, and his own personal jib throbbed with anticipation.
"Tom, what do you think?"

Tom opened the link and quickly scrolled the listing.
"Slav… it's amazing! The place is oozing with potential."
"That mid-century dormer window has left me dripping, that's for sure."
"And look at the size of that extension! Remind you of anyone? Me, perhaps…? It's what Belinda's book has been telling us to find. Something that needs renovation and for a reduced price."
Slavia felt ecstasy blooming between her legs like the yellow daffodils pictured in the listing on the front

patio of the bungalow, and she let out an involuntary moan.

"And that curved driveway... the exact same shape as your sex machine when at its most dangerous..." She licked her lips and stroked the cover of Belinda's book...

"Touch yourself for me, Tom."

Tom's panting was now almost as heavy as the machinery he'd just been operating. His own gear stick stood to attention, primed and ready to grind into action.

"Look at the floor plan, you filthy crane operator." Slavia purred in his ear.

His throbbing plank of flesh was harder than the original dark-wood floorboards in the bungalow hallway.

"I can't wait to paint your interior." Tom grunted into the phone.

"Before you do, I want you exposed like the brickwork on the living room chimney," Slavia retorted sexily.

Tom readily complied, turning towards the window of the crane, which was in full view of the town. He was now primed like a 1.7-litre kettle, full of hot liquid and ready to boil over.

Slavia's pleasure dome pulsated at the thought of him doing her bidding. That and the exquisite original copper kitchen worktops.

"And you know the best bit?" she whispered.

"What?" came the croaky reply.
"It's just within our budget."

With a cry, Tom exploded like a fork in a microwave, splattering the crane window with his own personal brand of creamy emulsion paint. A startled seagull that had been perched on the crane's arm squawked and took off into the air as Tom liberally decorated the crane's interior.
Still breathing heavily, he managed to gasp,
"Let's... book... viewing..." before falling back into his squishy fake leather seat.

Slavia salivated.

The next morning was thankfully a Saturday. It had been a pretty raunchy Friday night and they were feeling a little tired. That all changed when Tom rang the estate agent selling 'their' bungalow.
"Yes, sir, are you sure you really want to view this one? It's a bit quirky, so to speak." the agent tailed off despondently. This was the gazillionth enquiry for the property, and once punters looked round… well, they rarely came back.
"OK, I can do 11am today." he reluctantly agreed.
"Oh, and I'm Arthur, by the way."

Tom hung up and turned round to a still-naked Slavia, giving her the thumbs-up.
"Quirky," he said, "and cheaper… a great little renovation project."
"Sounds like our favourite type of sex… with all those rubber plugs and kitchen utensils."
"Why, Oh why, Tom, do you talk so sexy when I'm doing my toenails? Come on, let's get there before him and have a look round."

A quick thirty minutes later, they pulled up outside the bungalow… or rather what they thought was the bungalow. Much like a dishonest dating profile, it was now obvious the pictures had been taken some years ago when there had been an element of upkeep. Now the property was hidden behind large areas of pampas grasses, shrubbery and a massively out of control bush.

"Hello! Hello!" a voice called from the front door. The estate agent was smiling, pushing his way through the undergrowth to meet them.
"You pair are keen buyers, aren't you!" He opened the front door with a large set of brass keys, giving the phallic-looking knocker a loud bang for luck before ushering them inside.
Slavia's pelvic floor clenched in anticipation.

Arthur had just begun showing them round when his mobile rang. The conversation when he answered didn't sound friendly, and with an embarrassed look he put it on mute and said,
"Look, sorry... this is my boss and I've got to take it. It could take a while, so have a look around and I'll be outside if you need me."
They both nodded understandingly. His boss didn't sound in a good mood. Slavia thought she'd know her first port of call if Arthur turned up murdered in the next couple of weeks.

They quietly made their way over the threadbare carpets to the living room.
"God, Tom... just look at those pomegranate-shaped corbels... isn't that a sign of fertility?"
Tom looked around.

"Why not?" he thought, "no one will know…"
"Fertility, you say, Slavia… I'll give you fertility!" He promptly stripped off… everything. He sinuously approached Slavia, shaking his body like a dancing snake and murmuring strange words he'd never uttered before. The sexual magic of the house was so strong he couldn't contain himself.

"I want to redecorate your downstairs bathroom." he purred seductively.
"Then I'm going to refurbish your back doors and soak every single one of your hinges with my own special mixture of lubricating oil."
Slavia watched him, wide-eyed, as he silently tiptoed towards her, his girthy extension swinging hypnotically from side to side like a meaty metronome. He stopped in front of her and knelt down, peeling off the layers of her clothes until she was more than naked. He looked up at Slavia with a sly grin, taking a deep breath before plunging head first into her frothy love jacuzzi. As waves of pleasure rolled through her body, Slavia threw her head back. Her eyes widened further as she noticed the light fittings above her.

"Original fixtures," she moaned. The late 19th-century industrial salvage pendant lamp swung sexily in time as she thrust her flexible hips into Tom's now-glistening face. His tongue worked overtime as if it were on probation.

Slavia's orgasm was silently building, just like her excitement levels at glimpsing a marble-topped cast iron fireplace through one of the open bedroom doors.

"Open me up like the floor plan!" she suddenly howled, her fingers scrabbling against the very good imitation Victorian MDF skirting board. Tom shook his face from side to side like a Labrador after a dip in the local pond. His tongue danced across the folds of Slavia's love cave as he eagerly imagined the herb garden he could plant after all the rampant undergrowth had been removed.
Slavia was getting closer to her very own nirvana. She gripped onto Tom's hair for support and realized that his shaggy mane was almost identical to the medium-sized woollen rug she'd seen online. Her southern lips tingled as she imagined it paired with light-blue duck-egg painted cabinets.

Slavia's back arched dramatically as she convulsed onto Tom's face, almost breaking his larger-than-average nose with the force of her climax. The high ceilings reverberated reverently with her triumphant moaning.
"It's a good thing this place is semi-detached!" gasped Tom in awe.
"There's nothing 'semi' about that." Slavia giggled, gesturing to Tom's pulsating pecker.

But it would have to wait. The sound of Arthur's voice floated into earshot and Tom suddenly drooped in disappointment.

"At least Arthur will be getting lucky today." Slavia grinned as she urgently pulled her clothes back on.

"I think it's time we made an offer," Tom suggested. "How about £325,000? That's below their asking price."

"Belinda says they're used to negotiation... so let's do it!"

Slavia salivated;

Chapter 9;
The Survey;

Georgina Vulvana pressed the return key on her company laptop.

"Aggghhh," she sighed, her nightmare over at last. She'd just finally completed the property inspection and valuation report on a bungalow in Girthington-on-Sea. What should have been a half-day job had turned into almost three days of work, and her boss was not happy.

Her outbox pinged as the email was sent. She smiled. The property was finally off her books.

Meanwhile, across town, Slavia and Tom were feeling frustrated. After their offer had been accepted, they'd immediately initiated a full property survey for the bungalow on Throbberstead Avenue, but after many false promises, they still hadn't had the report back.

"Come on, Slav... we can't wait around here all day. Let's go for a walk in Girthington Woods behind the house and check out the local area one last time. I'll even buy you an ice cream!"

Twenty-three minutes later, ice-creams in hand, they were quietly strolling arm-in-arm through the shady woodland. It was sensually beautiful. As they reached a leafy and secluded area of the woods, Slavia's phone pinged.

"Tom!" she said breathlessly.

"It's here. The report... God, I feel weak at the knees."

"Sit down... here, underneath this tree. Read it out," Tom instructed.

"OK, here goes. Page one of sixty-nine.... sixty-nine pages!"

"Read it, Slav... don't jump to any conclusions just yet... remember Belinda's book."

But Slavia had a funny feeling of dread deep in her stomach. Even her most complicated fraud assessment documents only came to thirty-two pages.

"The bungalow grounds are heavily overgrown and no inspection could be made of the shed, driveway and boundary fencing." she read.
"Sounds like your delicious body right now. Can I have a peek?" Tom asked cheekily.

Slavia rolled her eyes and looked around, polishing off her cone before removing her blouse, skirt and thong. Apart from her boots, nothing else remained.
"Can you inspect and value this body, Mr Tom... or is it too overgrown? Like this bloody report?"
Tom drooled and let his chocolate ice-cream dribble down his denim shirt.
"Read on, Slav..."

"The internal pipe runs are all sagging and will need considerable uplifting if not complete replacement over the next six months." Slavia continued.
Tom felt his own pipe run spring into life – at least that was in fine working order. It strained against the fabric of his shorts, like an impatient plumber demanding immediate payment. He leaned forward and brushed his fingers along Slavia's inner thigh, causing her nipples to harden like twin-thread 42mm drywall screws.

Slavia sighed, opening her legs a little before continuing.
"Our surveyor notes that all the windows require extensive re-puttying and that the roof above the lounge will have to be replaced with thicker beams

to ensure structural integrity. Furthermore, the pine-stripped floorboards in the dining room will need to be replaced due to severe woodworm attack. Several walls will need some of the wall ties replacing. On the western side of the house the damp proof course will have to be renewed."

Slavia shook her head, realising that Tom was still fully dressed.

"Thomas, I think it's time you removed your shorts and boxers so I can properly assess *your* woodworm potential and damp proof course."

In no time at all, Tom's thick fleshy beam was waving lazily about in the summer breeze.

"I hope your load-bearing walls with their rusty wall ties are ready for me..." he growled.

"Yes," she muttered to herself as she straddled his throbbing pink love sword.

"But I believe there could be a water drainage problem here. Damp spots seem evident, that's for sure... ahhh!"

She gasped as he wriggled gently inside her.

"Oh God, Slav, your interior is glorious!" Tom cried as he thrust his hips like a dad dancing at a wedding.

"Although it feels like your damp-proof membrane is definitely compromised. It's a good thing I have my tools to hand."

"Shut up and ruin my structural integrity, you girthy cowboy builder," Slavia groaned, grinding her downstairs combi-boiler faster and faster.

They writhed around in the foliage like a snake wrestling a badger, Tom's ice-cream lying forgotten in a sensual puddle of melting chocolate and floating pheromones.
"Did you read anything about asbestos?" Tom grunted into Slavia's gaping earlobe, thrusting a little bit deeper with every syllable.
"It said the only health hazard we needed to worry about is the one between your legs." came the breathy response.

The pace of their passion increased until Slavia started to tremble.
"Tom… I… I think my hot water cylinder is about to blow."
"Only if my planning permission gets approved first, Mrs Slavia." he groaned.
"Oh, you do use such sexy language! I think I'm… I'm… SUBSIDING!"
With a wail of pleasure loud enough to wake Henry VIII himself, Slavia squirted like an ornate garden water feature.

Tom's axe-wielding orgasm sliced into him with the power of a Canadian lumberjack, and they collapsed together in the soft grass, completely spent and gasping for air.
After lying in blissful silence for a while, she smiled and scooped a glob of something out of Tom's hair.
"You, my boy, have a severe case of wet rot."

Tom laughed and sucked melted chocolate ice-cream off her finger with a terribly naughty gleam in his eye.

Slavia salivated;

They pulled on their clothing and left the woods arm-in-arm, primed and ready for the property completion they so desperately desired.

There was a flurry of activity once the property survey and the lawyer's searches had come back, and pretty soon contracts were exchanged.
'There's no going back now.' Slavia thought.
Bruce Clapworthy was true to his word: the agreed finances were in place for the day of completion.

The night before moving day, they were far too excited to sleep much. They woke up early, before driving Tom's work van full of all their worldly possessions over to the bungalow. After a takeaway flat white coffee and a flaccid-looking pair of croissants, they concentrated on the job at hand, shifting boxes and large packing crates full of God-knew-what into their new home.

As the last lumpy, love-stained box was carried inside, Slavia thirstily observed the throbbing forearm muscles standing out from Tom's sinuous body. She couldn't believe that she was now the proud owner of a beautiful bungalow as well as an above-averagely handsome and sexually virulent fiancé.
"I think it's about time we got our pleasure palace assembled," she said, nodding at the bed frame.

"Why don't you handle the erection whilst I find something to keep our mouths occupied?"

Thirty minutes of grunting, groaning and shoving later, the bed was in place and two large pizzas had been delivered: a Margarita for Tom and a Meat-Feast for Slavia. They sat cross-legged on their memory foam mattress, which had been extravagantly soaked in so many of their sexual secrets over the past year, and tucked in.

In no time at all, moving-day arousal had overtaken their hunger pangs, and the sticky mozzarella cheese acted as a lactose lubricant between their greasy bodies. Elastic strings of cheese dripped seductively down Slavia's lips and Tom did his best to suck them up with his surprisingly girthy tongue.
He wasn't particularly successful, but he did manage to unfasten the clasp on Slavia's bra in the process. Taking off his shirt, Tom smeared garlic dip onto his nipples, making them glisten like the new energy efficient screw-in light bulbs they'd installed in the bedroom lamps earlier that morning.

Without blinking, Slavia greedily started devouring his flavorsome pecs. Smacking her engorged lips in satisfaction.
"Mmm, that was delicious. If only we had something to drink."
Reaching into the bottom of the South American mahogany drawers that had been left behind by the

previous owner, Tom pulled out a bottle of vintage Aussie sparkling wine with a flourish.
"Ooohhhh!" squealed Slavia excitedly.
"You clever man, Tom. It's Swampy Creek Winery... my all-time fave!"

Tom smiled and poured them both a large glass of the sensuously frothing alcoholic liquid.
Slavia pulled at his waist and unbuckled his belt with a single sexy karate chop.
"You need stripping like the vinyl wallpaper in the spare bedroom." she intoned, like an impassioned vicar giving a sexy sermon.
"I demand that you give me every inch of my marital rights!"
Before he knew what was happening, Tom was completely naked, his knobly knees trembling with excitement.

"I hope your red oak banister is ready to be waxed, Mr Tom..." Scattering the pizza crusts aside, she opened her legs wide and drizzled a healthy glug of Aussie fizz all over her own swampy creek, as if seasoning a particularly luxurious salad. With her little finger she summoned Tom to bathe in his moist destiny.
He flexed his throbbing basement bicep, crawling towards Slavia's bubbly, furry igloo. Lathering himself in Swampy Creek, Tom looked straight into her green eyes before dipping into her fizzy depths.

With a scream of longing, Slavia bucked her hips and flipped herself over, sizzling like a hotdog, on a very hot barbecue. She was the one on top now, and Tom was at her undeniable mercy.

"Giddy-up, Mr. Tom," she whispered, before rhythmically grinding herself into his meaty cladding. Tom held onto her alpine breasts for dear life as Slavia picked up the pace and avalanched towards her snowy orgasm.

"Open me up like our old French windows, Tom! Plough me like a well-tended Anglian potato field." She stretched back and twisted her legs around him like an erotic pretzel, riding his fleshy saddle as if he were a fertile seahorse in mating season.

"Aggghhhh!" Tom howled as he lost control under Slavia's impassioned onslaught.

She added her cries of pleasure to his and together they shook their new bungalow to its sturdy 19th-century foundations.

As the Victorian dust settled, they lay together panting loudly like a pair of overheating laptops, basking in the post-orgasmic glow of their newly-christened bangalow.

"You definitely put the 'come' into completion," Tom sighed.

"Sssshhhh," Slavia replied dreamily. "Let me enjoy my fizz… sorry, your fizz."

Tom stretched languidly before slowly getting to his feet.

"Only five more rooms to go... Want to explore how sturdy those kitchen counters really are?"
Winking at her, he took a refreshing swig of sparkling wine and strutted out of the room.

Slavia observed him going, looking hungrily at the architectural curves of their bungalow and Tom's perfectly pert behind.
All mine, she thought happily.
And after everything they had been through, it finally was.
On the mantlepiece Belinda Blumenthal, Bella Ridley and Rocky Flintstone's book on,
"How to buy the best property for you."
Blinked back at her...

Slavia salivated.

Conclusion

So, Rocky and Bella, did you enjoy the story about my cousin Slavia and her partner Tom's house purchase adventure?

Bella replied, 'I didn't know you had a cousin Belinda… whatever next? But yes, they certainly followed OUR books advice and ended up buying their dream home. Wonderful.'

Rocky continued, 'So pleased for Slavia and Tom, do you think we'll get invited to the house warming party? Unfortunately, we're now at the end of this Life Tips so Belinda and Bella, what have you learned from all of this talk of purchasing the correct property for you?

Belinda replied,
'Research… research… research;'
And Bella followed up,
'Location… location… location;'

Good! Well done and what is your first parameter?

Belinda replied,
'Choose the area where you want to be;'
Bella added,
'Purchase in the best area you can afford;'

Excellent, well done and what must we do to make
these things happen?

Belinda thought hard and said,
'Ground search continually to find the right location;
Bella too thought for a second,
'Don't get stuck in a declining area, this is the worst
mistake you can make;'

Yes, well done and never forget you can change the
property but not the area OK;

Belinda continued now into the stride of the thing,
'Try to find undervalued properties;'
Bella squeaked,
'You'll make money when you buy right just like your
cous, Slavia;'

Good answers, and remember to think ahead to your
future needs;

Belinda chorused,
'Choose a house or an apartment to suit you;'

Bella added thoughtfully,
'It's your choice, make the correct one.'

Well, I am amazed that you pair have retained so
much of my words... now quick test... what is a wall
tie? They got mentioned in the story after all!
No!!! only joking!

So, guys, I'll see you in a few weeks when we'll do
our next Life Tips for Belinkers!
Ciao for now!

'Ciao Rocky!' said Bella.
'Ciao Rocky!' said Belinda, 'See you soon!'

Remember to always take the correct specialist advice and obtain the relevant planning permissions and building regulations for your part of the world.